Pebble®
Plus

Cycles of Nature

The Water Cycle

A 4D Book

by Catherine Ipcizade

Consultant: Dr. Sandra F. Mather, Professor Emerita
Department of Earth and Space Sciences
West Chester University, West Chester, Pa.

PEBBLE
a capstone imprint

Download the Capstone 4D app!

- Ask an adult to download the Capstone 4D app.

- Scan the cover and stars inside the book for additional content.

When you scan a spread, you'll find fun extra stuff to go with this book! You can also find these things on the web at www.capstone4D.com using the password: water.00399

Pebble Plus is published by Pebble
1710 Roe Crest Drive, North Mankato, Minnesota 56003
www.mycapstone.com

Library of Congress Cataloging-in-Publication Data
Library of Congress Cataloging-in-Publication data is available on the Library of Congress website.
ISBN 978-1-9771-0039-9 (library binding)
ISBN 978-1-9771-0043-6 (paperback)
ISBN 978-1-9771-0047-4 (eBook PDF)
Summary: Lakes evaporate. Clouds form from condensation. Rain falls and fills rivers and lakes. Soak up facts about the water cycle and why we need to keep water clean.

Editorial Credits
Emily Raij, editor; Charmaine Whitman, designer;
Eric Gohl, media researcher; Kris Wilfahrt, production specialist

Image Credits
Newscom: Blend Images/Ariel Skelley, 21; Shutterstock: aekikuis, 5, Alexey Osokin, cover (left), 1 (left), Eakachai Leesin, 17, FenlioQ, 7, Firstyahoo, cover (bottom), 1 (bottom), Kuzmenko Viktoria, 10, Neirfy, 15, Ostariyanov, 9, pixy_nook, 11, Rich Carey, 19, Serkan Senturk, 13, Zhivka Kalinkova, cover (right), 1 (right)
Design Elements: Shutterstock

Note to Parents and Teachers

The Cycles of Nature set supports the national science standards related to patterns in the natural world. This book describes and illustrates the water cycle. The images support early readers in understanding the text. The repetition of words and phrases helps early readers learn new words. This book also introduces early readers to subject-specific vocabulary words, which are defined in the Glossary section. Early readers may need assistance to read some words and to use the Table of Contents, Glossary, Read More, Internet Sites, Critical Thinking Questions, and Index sections of the book.

Printed and bound in China.
309

Table of Contents

The Water Cycle

Grab an umbrella! It's going to rain! A thick cloud moves by. Why does this change in weather happen? It's because of the water cycle!

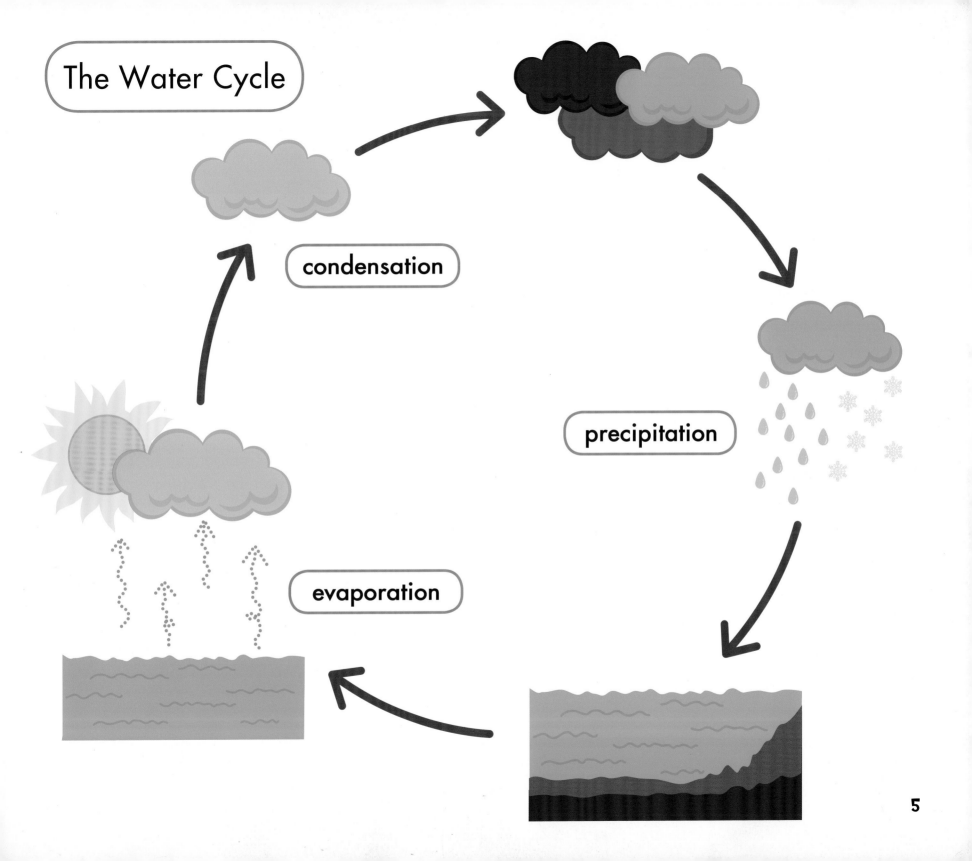

The Water Cycle

condensation

precipitation

evaporation

5

Liquid to Gas

Imagine a lake in summer.
Heat from the sun warms
the water. Warm water rises
in the air and turns into gas.

The gas is vapor.
This process is called
evaporation.
Water evaporates on
plant leaves too.

Clouds at Work

Vapor from lakes and oceans cools. It turns into tiny water droplets. This is called condensation, which makes clouds or dew.

dew

Clouds are made of water droplets. The droplets become too heavy. That's when rain or snow falls. This is called precipitation.

precipitation

From Water to Ice

Precipitation falls into lakes and oceans. Water can also freeze into ice in cold weather. The water cycle starts again when it gets warm.

People and Water

The water cycle has repeated for billions of years. Our water has been on Earth a long time. We drink the same water the first people on Earth drank!

If we dump chemicals
and trash into the water,
we make water dirty.
This is called pollution.

Dirty water is dangerous
to drink. It can change
what lives and grows in places
too. We need to work to keep
our water clean.

Glossary

condensation—changing from a gas to a liquid

dew—small water droplets that collect overnight on outside surfaces, such as plant leaves

evaporation—changing from a liquid to a gas

pollution—materials that hurt Earth's water, air, and land

precipitation—water that falls from clouds to Earth's surface; precipitation can be rain, hail, sleet, or snow.

vapor—a gas made from a liquid or a solid

weather—the condition outdoors at a certain time and place; weather changes with each season.

Read More

Maloof, Torrey. *Water Cycle*. Science Readers: Content and Literacy. Huntington Beach, Calif.: Teacher Created Materials, 2015.

Olien, Rebecca. *The Water Cycle at Work*. Water in Our World. North Mankato, Minn.: Capstone Press, 2016.

Stewart, Melissa. *Water*. National Geographic Readers. Washington, D.C.: National Geographic Children's Books, 2014.

Internet Sites

Use FactHound to find Internet sites related to this book.

Visit www.facthound.com

Just type in 9781977100399 and go.

 Super-cool stuff! Check out projects, games and lots more at **www.capstonekids.com**

Critical Thinking Questions

1. Why doesn't water evaporate as much during the winter?

2. Why does it rain?

3. How can people help keep water clean?

Index